*To valiant underdogs and underhorses everywhere—*
*and to my dad, who played the ponies*
*—A.B.*

*For my dad, Thomas L. Szalay,*
*who continued to cheer us on*
*—D.S.*

**Artie Bennett** is an executive copy editor by day and a writer by night. He is the author of several popular children's picture books, as well as two riotous joke and riddle books. When Artie stumbled on the story of Zippy Chippy, he found himself champing at the bit to introduce young readers to this remarkable, inspiring tale of whoa! He lives with his wife in Brooklyn, New York, where he spends his spare time searching for a parking space. Visit ArtieBennett.com . . . before someone else does!

"It appears there is no topic Mr. Bennett can't make funny and educational."
*—The Huffington Post*

**Dave Szalay** is an award-winning illustrator, aspiring author, and college professor. Dave, his wife, and three cats live along a stream that runs through the nearby Cuyahoga Valley National Park in Ohio. They have two adult sons and a granddaughter. Visit DaveSzalay.com for more information.

Jacket photo of Zippy Chippy copyright © 2020 by Artie Bennett
Text copyright © 2020 by Artie Bennett
Illustrations copyright © 2020 by Dave Szalay

First published in the United States, Great Britain, Canada, Australia,
and New Zealand in 2020 by NorthSouth Books Inc.,
an imprint of NordSüd Verlag AG, CH-8050 Zürich, Switzerland.

Distributed in the United States by NorthSouth Books Inc., New York 10016.
Library of Congress Cataloging-in-Publication Data is available.
ISBN: 978-0-7358-4396-7
Printed in Latvia, by Livonia Print, Riga
1 3 5 7 9 · 10 8 6 4 2
www.northsouth.com

# The True Story of ZIPPY CHIPPY
## The Little Horse That Couldn't

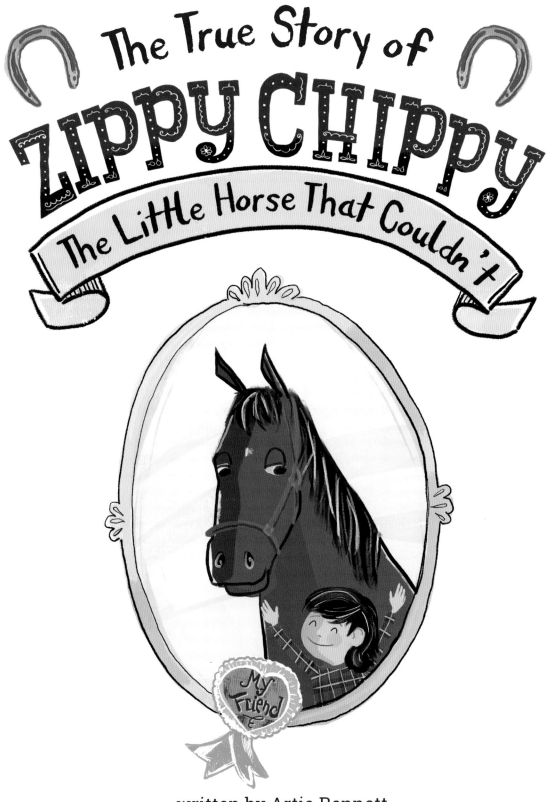

My Friend

written by Artie Bennett

illustrated by Dave Szalay

North South

1917 Man o' War 1947

1934 War Admiral 1959

1954 Bold Ruler 1971

BEST

1

WIN

TOP PRIZE

1

NUMBER ONE

**ZIPPY CHIPPY** was a racehorse, descended from legends that ran like the wind.

He was destined for glory—and would follow in their hoofbeats.

The only problem was, when Zippy ran . . .

. . . it was more like a gentle breeze.
When the starting bell rang, instead of running,
Zippy sometimes stood perfectly still.

His owner didn't give up!

There was greatness in Zippy's bloodlines and power in his pedigree.

Zippy was a thoroughbred, through and through.

But when he raced at Belmont Park—home to the
Belmont Stakes, the third jewel in the famed Triple Crown—
Zippy stopped right in the middle of the track. What lovely
smells were wafting in the air that afternoon.

Zippy was also a devilish prankster. He would stick his tongue out at people . . . and snatch the hats off passersby (returning them partly chewed).

Zippy continued to lose—nineteen races in a row.

And his owner finally called it quits!

But *who* would want a racehorse that didn't win?

Felix Monserrate—a horse trainer from Puerto Rico—
was that someone.

Felix traded his old pickup truck, with nearly 200,000
miles on it, for Zippy Chippy.

Felix believed in Zippy and felt he just needed the
right trainer—*himself!*—to bring out the horse's potential.
*He* would make Zippy a star.

But Felix soon found out that Zippy was trouble. With a capital *T*!

He trashed the exercise barn and bit his new trainer. He bucked his riders and then trotted home by himself.

The rambunctious horse once even clamped on to Felix's shirt and dangled him in the air.

Zippy was also an accomplished escape artist. He had a Houdini-like ability to break out of his stall. It was only when a full metal screen was installed over his stall door that these shenanigans stopped.

The horse with the donkey-like ears could also be stubborn as a mule. If Zippy didn't want to do something, he didn't.

He was so ornery, they kept him in an area that was off limits to most everyone for safety's sake.

Felix was wondering if he had made a big mistake . . .

But when Felix's eight-year-old daughter, Marisa,
went missing . . . Felix finally found her in Zippy's
stall, being nuzzled by the temperamental horse.

From then on, Felix said, "He's like a member of the family."

Fast friends, Marisa and Zippy enjoyed many spirited games of hide-and-seek together.

Like Felix, Zippy had a sweet tooth—and a fondness for chocolate, cupcakes, doughnuts, jelly beans, and ice cream. Felix would feed him peppermint candies before a race.

Competing now in the Finger Lakes area, having been banished to second-rate tracks, Zippy lost the next *seventy* straight races, the track record!

He might have lost more, but he was banned from racing—after failing to leave the starting gate *three* times in a row at the sound of the bell.

A ban from one racetrack translated into a ban from *all* racetracks.

Poor Zippy had nowhere to run.

Did Felix give up?

No! After a year of looking, Felix found a track in Northampton, Massachusetts, willing to let Zippy pursue his passion, and his dreams.

As Zippy was coming up on eighty career races, Felix decided to retire his horse, to put him out to pasture.

But Zippy bridled at the change. He became depressed and stopped eating when he wasn't racing. Felix *had* to bring Zippy back to the track. Zippy loved being a racehorse. It was in his blood. He just wasn't terribly good at it.

Zippy lost many more races, and in 1999, he broke the record for most consecutive losses, eighty-six, without a win.

"Not everybody can be a winner," Felix would tell reporters, with massive understatement.

But as Zippy's losses continued to mount, a strange thing happened.

People started to take notice of the hapless horse who had never posed in the winner's circle. Sportswriters popped up. Crowds came to cheer on Zippy, just like they did for his champion ancestors. *And* they bet on Zippy to win.

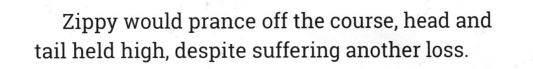

Zippy would prance off the course, head and tail held high, despite suffering another loss.

Felix felt that Zippy needed a win—*any* win—
to boost his morale.

So, in August 2000, he set up a race against a
minor-league baseball player. The scoreboard
trumpeted "Man Against Beast."

But Zippy, true to form, lost once more—beaten
by the outfielder in the forty-yard sprint!

Felix tried everything to change Zippy's luck— different saddles, different jockeys, shorter races, longer workouts . . .

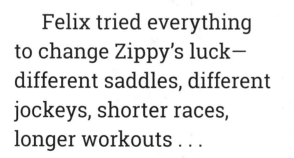

. . . even different feed!

Horseshoes are said to bring good luck . . . but not on Zippy!

"We may be down, but we ain't done," Felix said.

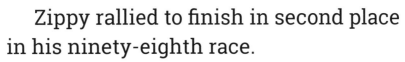

Zippy rallied to finish in second place in his ninety-eighth race.

But in his 100th race, in September 2004, Zippy would finish dead last.

Though not before a remarkable farewell act . . .

When the bell rang and the race began, Zippy stopped momentarily to bow to the crowd.

It was a fitting—and heartfelt—gesture, and brought tears to many eyes. And it was now time for the winless wonder to call it quits.

If Zippy had earned a single win in his career—he finished 0–100—he would have been just another bad racehorse. But because he lost every one, he's a legend, too. Just like his fabled ancestors.

It takes guts to compete—win, lose, or draw. And it takes courage to dream. Zippy showed us that you can lose and lose and lose and *still* be a winner. Yep, Zippy won in the end.

YIPPEE, ZIPPY CHIPPY!!!

# Author's Note

Apparently, Zippy Chippy acquired his delightful name by surprise. Breeders submit three prospective names to the Jockey Club when registering a horse. So, along with two rather conventional ones, the breeder submitted the name Zippy Chippy, which was what his small daughter called the horse. He never imagined the registry would opt for the zaniest of the three, but they did.

When Felix obtained Zippy, he also saved the horse's life. Zippy was about to be auctioned off to a slaughterhouse (in Canada or Mexico), where horses are turned into steaks and sold to Europeans with a taste for horsemeat.

There is a saying heard among people in the racing business: "Better not to love a horse." That's because racehorses are a costly investment and are sold off when their value decreases—or increases. Sometimes they even have to be put down. Owners need to keep their emotional distance. They know it's a business. But Zippy's situation was very different. This horse with attitude was loved.

One year after Zippy lost his much-ballyhooed race with the baseball player, he would take sweet revenge, vanquishing a different, less fleet-footed ballplayer in a fifty-yard dash. The longer course gave Zippy a chance to add a little horsepower and pick up some speed.

Because of off-track betting, you didn't even have to be at the racetrack to bet on Zippy, and fans across the country ponied up. (In fact, so many people bet on Zippy to win that he often ran as a favorite, *despite* his monumental lack of success!) Spectators besieged Felix for his autograph. Even *People* magazine profiled Zippy in May 2000, posing him alongside a tortoise. Zippy Chippy had developed a cult following.

Some horses are retrained for riding programs after their racing days are past. Zippy, though, had a brief career as an outrider pony. Outrider ponies escort other horses in the post parade, when the horses make their way to the starting gate past the grandstands before the race begins, following the bugler's call to post. This second career was cut short when Zippy reverted to his earlier habit of biting the other horses.

Felix and Zippy would be together for about fifteen years. In April 2010, he sold Zippy to Old Friends, a retirement facility for former racehorses, yesterday's heroes, after being assured that Zippy would live out his days in comfort. He would be housed at Old Friends at Cabin Creek Farm, in Greenfield Center, New York. The farm is just northwest of Saratoga Springs, home to the country's third-oldest racetrack.

In the summer of 2012, Old Friends made Zippy an ambassador. He went on tour in Kentucky bluegrass country to call attention to the need for humane treatment of aging racehorses, who were no longer able to compete or to breed. As always, Zippy enjoyed the spotlight.